The Seven Essential Skills Needed to Survive a Deadly Attack

In the Game of Life and Death Winning isn't Everything. It's the Only Thing.

Writings of Purpose and Intent

By

Ernest Emerson

Copyright © 2015 Ernest Emerson

All rights reserved. No part of this book may be reproduced, stored in a retrieval system, or transcribed, in any form or by any means, electronic, mechanical, photocopying, recording or otherwise without written permission of the author.

ISBN-13: 978-1506026510

ISBN-10: 1506026516

About the author:
Ernest Emerson is the founder and owner of the company, Emerson Knives, Inc. and is considered, "The Father of Tactical Knives," having designed the most iconic and well known combat knives in history.

He is a Black Belt Hall of Fame member and United States Martial Arts Hall of Fame Member and is a "Tier One" hand-to-hand combat and edged weapons instructor who has taught his combat system to many of the world's most deadly warriors, including the U.S. Navy SEAL Teams, U.S. Marines, U.S. Army Special Forces and various Government agencies.

Sir Ernest Emerson is a Knight of The Noble Order of the Black Shamrock and also holds the coveted title of Master-at-Arms. He is a noted lecturer, author and is an expert witness for the Los Angeles District Attorney's Office in deadly force cases. He has appeared on many T.V. shows, radio programs and has acted as a technical expert on numerous award winning movies.

His background includes playing professional baseball, boxing, Jeet Kune Do and Gracie Jiu Jitsu. He is the founder of The Emerson Combat System and is the owner of the Black Shamrock Combat Academy in Los Angeles, California.

He is the husband of a beautiful wife and the father to three wonderful children. Mr. Emerson is a Rock n' Roll junkie and enjoys the taste of fine scotch whiskey. He may be contacted at info@emersonknives.com.

Dedication

Dedicated to all those who know that our fight has just begun and stand ready and willing to sacrifice everything to preserve our way of life. There is no higher calling.

Disclaimer

Please note that the author is NOT RESPONSIBLE in any manner whatsoever for any injury that may result from practicing the techniques and/or following the instructions given within. Since the physical activities described herein may be too strenuous in nature for some readers to engage in safely, it is essential that a physician be consulted prior to training.

Table of Contents

Introduction...8

Chapter 1- Situational Awareness....................17
Never Leave Home without It.

Chapter 2- Preemptive Self Defense................27
Stopping Danger before It Starts.

Chapter 3- Your Gut Never Lies........................35
If There is Any Doubt-There's No Doubt.

Chapter 4- The Will to Survive..........................40
Second Place Is Last Place and in This Case, Second Place Is the Morgue.

Chapter 5- Fight for Your Life............................45
Make My Kids Orphans or His Kids Orphans?

Chapter 6- Loss of Self..51
Lose Yourself to Win the Fight.

Chapter 7- Never do Anything Without a Purpose Never Do Anything That Is Useless...................60

Conclusion...64

Emerson's Commandments of A Warrior

1. Protect the weak
2. Defend the innocent
3. Standup to tyranny and unjust behavior
4. Take responsibility for your actions and be prepared to accept the consequences
5. Honor friendship with loyalty
6. Stand tall in the face of adversity
7. Ask more of yourself than others
8. Never do anything without a purpose
9. Never do anything that is useless
10. Be honest in your intentions and actions with everyone you meet

Introduction

The lights are bright, the cheers and whistles of the crowd have a strange rhythmic ebb and flow and to you it sounds a little like you're hearing it all through a long cardboard tube. You're in a light sweat. The gate behind you swings shut and you look up towards the cheers, but can see nothing because of the spotlights pointed, it seems, directly at you. Your mind is racing, but you are focused.

Your hands tremble slightly and you begin to breathe deep and heavy to get more oxygen into your body. You can actually feel your heart beat faster and faster. Looking across the ring you see him.

He looks mad, focused and intense, hopping from one foot to the other in the universal rhythm known only to fighters. Your mind screams, I'm Ready! I'm Ready! I am Ready!" The ref shouts "Fighters touch gloves!" It breaks your concentration and you step forward to the center of the ring.

Or:

It's 10:30 PM and as you turn down the street to your apartment, you notice there are no parking spots out front.

"I know it's late, but can't there just be one open spot that isn't a block away? Wait a minute there's one" Looking at the spot, it does look tight but you know you can fit. As you jockey the car back and forth your thoughts go to work and your boss.

"Whenever Tom is absent the boss always yells at *us*. We're not the one who's absent. Why doesn't he yell at Tom?" You open the door reaching across the seat for your briefcase and step out.

"By the time that jerk Tom shows up back to work, everything has calmed down. This is the fourth time it's happened. The boss is a . . ." **Wham!**

It's not a noise, but a blinding flash of white light that drops you to your knees. Your right hand shoots reflexively to the back of your head. Something hits you explosively in the middle of your back and drives your face hard into the pavement. You hear something. It's not a voice; it's more like a snarl crossed with a grunt, not really even human sounding. It's getting louder – each time you are hit. Again and again something explodes into the side of your face and ribs. Three more times something slams down between your shoulder blades and grinds you into the cold blacktop. Finally the crushing blows stop and you hear footsteps, running footsteps, and the world fades to black.

Two Different Fights – Two Different Worlds.
Which one are you preparing for?

There are many of us who readily accept our role as protector and defender of the things that we cherish and love: our wives, our husbands, our children, our family, our neighbors, our teammates, and our country. And those of us who have consciously decided to accept that responsibility have taken steps to insure that we are able to do so effectively. But have they been the right steps? Now think of this: "Danger strikes when you least expect it." What happens if you are not there? At that moment, your wife, your daughter, your son, or a complete stranger may be the only protector in the game.

They may have no one but themselves to rely on. So many times I have heard the statement, "My family is safe. I've trained at this shooting school, this martial arts school, etc." Well, don't kid yourself. Unless you and your family are aware of how to survive a real, deadly attack, then you are still unprepared. This book will outline seven essential skills to help you and your family survive.

Let's look at it like this: Let's say I trained an athlete how to hit a baseball and hit it well. Let's say I even trained him well enough to hit against major league pitching. You could say he's a really good hitter. Why just look at all the training he's had! But let's say I never taught him a thing about the game of baseball. Let's say I get him up to bat and he punches a line drive out to left field...and then he just stands there. Players, fans, and coaches are screaming at him. Run! Run! Run! Run? Where? Why? And he is thrown out at first on the relay from left field. He has all the skills needed to hit. He knows how to run. But he never learned anything more than to hit the ball, or maybe in your case, hit the target.

You might be able to hit the target, but are you ready to play the game? Take notice that the title of this book is, "The Seven Essential Skills Needed to Survive a Deadly Attack." You will notice that the words win, beat, prevail, dominate, subdue or outscore are not in the title. You win at checkers. You outscore your opponent in basketball. In fact if you strip out all the unnecessary words from the title, only three will remain. And those three words are Essential to Survive. Nothing--repeat, nothing, else matters. A deadly attack is not a game. There is no winner or loser.

The very nature of what I'm discussing here is simple. If a deadly attack is successful, someone lives and someone dies. If you start to look at it in those terms, you start to see the possible outcomes. If you can do that, you can prepare to create the outcomes that will be in your favor.

For example, if I realize that I'm walking into a trap, then turn around and make an exit, I have created an outcome in my favor. I didn't even mess up a hair on my head. And the bad guy(s) who set the trap may not have messed up their hair either--but, who cares? I did what was needed to survive. Surviving a deadly attack does not always mean engaging in that attack or becoming a willing or non-willing participant.

You will find that throughout this book, and in all the other books I've written, I will ask the reader/student (it's the same in my classes) to accept a premise. I don't ask you to understand it or to question it. I ask you to accept it, lock, stock, and barrel. Why? Because I'm bringing to you a lifetime of experience in these subjects. This experience has taught me that there are some universal truths, principles, and laws that exist in all endeavors. It sometimes takes a lifetime of study to self-discover them. I'm giving you the benefit of my experience to shorten your journey in discovering these truths. Asking you to blindly accept a premise is a teaching methodology that I use to shorten the learning process. It puts everyone on the same page as I explain/teach various aspects of human conflict and it has proven to be very effective. If I'm doing my job, you should end up agreeing with the premise, when I'm through explaining the process.

Some of these truths I learned, and some were taught to me by those much wiser than myself. So here is the first universal truth. It is one of the most important truths and it is one of the most important things I have ever learned.

It consists of two parts.

Part 1: Every skill is a skill that has been learned.

Part 2: Any skill that can be learned is a skill that can be taught.

Mozart was not born knowing how to play an instrument. Einstein wasn't born knowing physics and Babe Ruth wasn't born knowing how to hit a baseball. By whatever set of circumstances, they all *learned* how to do what they did best. It is the same with the skills and strategies you need to survive a deadly attack. You may also find that you can apply the strategies as defined in this book to a number of circumstances such as business, sports, martial arts, or even marriage, but none of these bear the consequences of a *deadly* attack. So, for the sake of what I'm about to outline in this book I will always be talking in terms of responding to a deadly attack: a form of combat where the attacker, the bad guy wants to and intends to kill you or your loved ones. In this case, your goal is to survive by any means necessary, whether by use of intuition, awareness, ruthlessness, violence, cunning, and guile, or simply just running like hell. Your goal is to survive. If that means killing the bad guy, so be it. If that means outrunning the bad guy, so be it. If you are the survivor of a deadly attack, I guess you *could* call yourself the winner.

Here's the way we are going to approach this: A bad guy is going to kill you or your loved ones and you must stop him from accomplishing his goal. That's what this book is all about.

Chapter 1

Situational Awareness

"I Never Saw It Coming."

What is Situational Awareness? Situational awareness means you never want to be the one to say, "I never saw it coming." What is situational awareness? Situational awareness is a working blend of preparation and training, knowledge of the environment, perceptual alertness and instinct-- gut feel.

For example, in my world I am always scanning the environment. I never sit with my back to the entrance. I always look for potential cover and alternate escape routes. I am always scanning the crowd in theaters, restaurants, and airplanes, actually anywhere and everywhere I am. And yes, I am always armed. You may think my behavior somewhat extreme.

But aren't you also already using situational awareness? Maybe not to the same degree as some of us, but I bet you are. Do you drive a car? When you are driving your car are you looking ahead, down the road?

Do you check your rear view mirror? Are you looking at other cars, other drivers, assessing their driving, anticipating their actions? Are you aware of your speed, covering your brakes, and slowing down when you see brake lights going on ahead? I bet you can answer yes to all of these questions.

So I am going to tell you one thing and then I'm going to ask you one thing. You *are* already practicing situational awareness, probably every day. Now I'll ask the question, why are you only doing it when you are on the freeway? Ninety-five percent of your life, you are not in your car. Now I am going to hit you with a dose of sober, hard truth. Whether you are aware of it or not, you can figure that you are *always* being scanned by someone of bad intent as to whether or not you would be an easy victim. That's not being paranoid. That's a fact. Believe that it is true every time you are in a public place.

I have two beautiful blonde daughters. How many times a week do you think I talk to them about situational awareness? I have always told them, "Remember, in every bar or club that you go into, there is at least one bad guy in the room. And that guy is looking for a victim and he will check you out. He may not get you. He may not get anyone that night or even the next. But eventually he will, given the right circumstances, the right opportunity and the *right victim*. You might ask, "Aren't you being a little extreme? Aren't you being a little paranoid?" Is being prepared being paranoid?

Only if you're preparing for an attack by Martians.

How do you prevent yourself from becoming that "right victim"? At this point it is relevant to mention one of the best training aids in modern operational skills training, Colonel Jeff Cooper's color code system of human awareness. Colonel Cooper developed the system as a visual and mental aid in raising levels of awareness and preparedness training for soldiers getting ready to go into battle. Briefly, Colonel Coopers color code is as follows:

Condition White–You are unprepared and unready to take lethal action. If you are attacked in condition white you will probably die unless your adversary is totally inept.

Condition Yellow–You bring yourself to the understanding that your life may be in danger and you may have to do something about it.

Condition Orange--You have determined upon a specific adversary and are prepared to take action, which may result in his death, but you are not in a lethal mode.

Condition Red—You are in a lethal mode and will shoot if circumstances warrant it.

In terms of situational awareness, it is your duty to yourself, your loved ones, your teammates, or those under your command, to always be situationally aware and never ever caught with your guard down. Using Coopers color code can help you carry out that duty.

Like every other skill we are discussing in this book, situational awareness is a learned skill. And like every other skill, it does take practice and time to make it part of your everyday routine. Besides that, it is actually fun to observe the world around you, especially with a conscious, analytical awareness. Open up your eyes. Pay attention to what's going on around you. You'll be surprised at what you see, and it just may save your life.

Situational awareness can be described as an active awareness of your physical environment and any individuals within that environment that have the ability, means, or motive to interact with you in any way, whether it is friendly, benign or with bad intent. It is 360 degrees of consciousness and awareness that extends out from you at the center at least 20 to 30 feet, at all times.

A mantra that we have all seen on posters, placed on trains, at airports, in subways, and on buses "If you see something, say something," is a perfect embodiment of encouraging situational awareness in the general public. The poster is asking you to become aware, to look around, be vigilant, so you will notice the abandoned suitcase or backpack or perhaps the suspicious or nervous individual who just doesn't seem right.

Situational awareness in a non-threatening environment is a little different than in a known, dangerous environment. Let's look at a simple progression to illustrate some points and how they apply;

1. You are at a family reunion and after dinner, you and all of your cousins and their wives migrate to a local bar for some laughter, beer, and pool. You are leaving a

known safe environment, home with family, and entering a familiar but unknown, environment at least in terms of danger.

2. When you get to the bar you park down the street in a public parking lot and walk up and into the bar. There are only 4 other people inside the bar, two couples sitting at a table in the bar, also enjoying a Friday night out in the town. You notice them as you walk in but they pay no attention to you other than a casual glance as your party of 10 comes into the bar. You glance around the bar looking into all the "dark "corners to see if there is anyone "lurking" in the shadows. Seeing that it is "safe," you loosen up a little and get ready to enjoy your family's company. You are not worried about anyone in your family, so you're not too concerned about being close to them, (within arm's reach). And you hope that if something does go south that at least one of your party will notice it and alert the pack. In terms of situational awareness, you are in a state of **"relaxed readiness**."

3. Suddenly a group of 8 Outlaw Bikers enter the bar. You are instantly aware of this new presence. You immediately begin to assess them and their state of behavior. Are they intoxicated? Rowdy, ornery, etc.?

And you observe their interaction with the bartender for any other signs of unusual or bad behavior. They seem content to just order their beers and move over to a table in the corner away from the exit. You in turn make sure that there is a clear path to the back door. You decide to be aware of them but do not interact with them in any way. There's no need to say hello, nod or do anything to draw attention to yourself. You do make a conscious decision to leave if they get rowdy and you do not let any of them get close to you without being acutely aware of their presence and actions. For instance, when you have to go up to the bar to order some drinks, you also make a note not to let any of them get between you, your party, and the back exit, your only clear avenue of escape. It is a potentially volatile situation, but no need to act until circumstances change to warrant it. After about an hour you and your family decide that it's time to leave the bar. You all walk toward the front door, past the bikers who pay no attention to you or your party. As to situational awareness, you were in a state of **"heightened vigilance."**

4. As you leave the bar you see a crowd on the sidewalk out front and you hear loud shouting, cursing, and swearing. There's obviously a confrontation taking place

and suddenly it breaks out into a fight between two males. There are about 20 people directly in front of you and your party and without warning another fight breaks out between several of those 20 others. You have now entered an active, dangerous environment and you have switched to a state of **"hyper-vigilance."** Not you or any of your party are involved or engaged in the melee, but one wrong decision could thrust you into the fray.

Quickly you scan for anyone near your party and whether they present as a threat or non-threat. Then you look for the path of least resistance, the easiest way out of the proximity to the danger and you move in that direction, guiding your party with you. "But the car's this way," someone says, pointing past the crowd. "Follow me," you state clearly and you lead them down the block and out of danger. You cross over the street and turn back to travel the rest of the block back to where the cars are parked. As you reach them you hear, "What's wrong, Bob? I wanted to see who was going to win. I thought you were a tough guy. You scared of a bunch of punks? I'm not. I can handle myself, right honey?" your cousin speaks boldly. Then suddenly Bang!...Bang!...Bang! And you hear screams from the crowd down the street. And then everyone knows you made the right decision.

So as you can see there are varying degrees of situational awareness that are at times, dictated by both the environment and the circumstances you find yourself in. And that environment can change, fluctuate and demand a conscious hand on the volume control of your vigilant state as it can transform dramatically from moment to moment. It must be noted that situational awareness, in regard to your "read" of an environment, is also influenced by your own historical perspective and life experience. In other words, the level of situational awareness of a Marine just back from Afghanistan will be much different than that of a Sociology professor from the local university. Or, the situational awareness of an undercover DEA agent will be quite different than that of a Journalism professor from the local university. Sorry about my dig at the intellectual elite. No, I'm not really sorry. But, if you are one of those who believe that all people are good by nature, then at some point in time, you're going to get your ass handed to you.

You must accept the fact that there are good guys and that there are bad guys out there. If you do accept that, then you will more easily assess individuals in terms of threat/non threat. This may represent a paradigm shift for some and no shift at all for others. All of us fall somewhere in between both of these extremes. It is a matter of degrees of awareness that you assign to any environment you enter that determines how switched on you need to be.

However, at a baseline state of 360 degrees, situational awareness must be constant and maintained so that if any situation escalates into the danger zone, you are not caught off guard. You are prepared to act and that you never, ever need to say these words, "I never saw it coming."

Chapter 2

Preemptive Self Defense

Stopping Danger Before it starts.

One of the first steps to understanding the concept of pre-emptive self-defense is to become familiar with the predator/prey relationship. And the first step to understanding that relationship is to accept that we are an animal just the same as a lion, a mouse, an alligator or an elephant. We may be man. We may have a soul and we may be a higher being, but we are still an animal. If you accept that premise, then you can understand much better what I'm about to describe.

Secondly, if you accept that premise, you will see that certain principles apply to the interaction of predator and prey and they are the same principles for all creatures from insects to human beings. You can read more about the *Strategy of Principles,* in one of my other books, "The Seven Strategies of Hand to Hand Combat." For the sake of this conversation, I'm going to ask you to also accept another premise. One that states that a principle is a principle and it doesn't care where it is applied. It is a universal truth that is indiscriminate in its application and it is always in play. So if I know the dynamics of a predator/prey relationship and the principles that are triggered, then I can identify them, which allows me to prepare for them, train for them, manipulate them, employ them, or avoid them. It is important to understand that *no one* can prepare for what he doesn't know.

There has always been a lot of information available from many sources about how to avoid becoming a victim. Not as much has been written, taught, or discussed about being the predator, when in fact they are two sides of the same coin. One cannot exist without the other. A simple analogy would be that of a football team that practices with no idea or Intel about the team they are going to play next. You can practice and master all kinds of wonderful plays and defense, but if your opponents step onto the field and they are all eight feet tall, weigh four hundred pounds, and can run like Olympic Spartans, all of a sudden you're going to get caught pretty unprepared.

From the predator point of view I am going to name a couple of the better known apex predators. Consider the tiger, the lion, and the alligator, top apex predators in their domains. They all have a combination of traits in common. The predator is governed by a number of principles that are designed by evolution to ensure the survival of their species. In elegant simplicity it boils down to a simple equation. It is a balance of energy, how much energy is expended to capture the food (energy) and how much energy the catch (the prey) will provide. Averaged over period of time, if the balance of the equation is in favor of the amount of energy gained by the predator from the prey, the predator will survive. And if it is tipped in favor of the prey, the predator will starve. You will note that in nature, there are no obese predators. So in reality, odds of the average predator/prey eqution must be pretty slim.

In order to tip the balance in the predator's favor just enough for survival, the predator must use strategies and tactics that allow it to accomplish its goal efficiently. All of the top of the line apex predators are ambush predators. In fact almost all predators use the *ambush* as the cornerstone or foundation of their predatory strategy. In order to facilitate the ambush, several tactics are employed.

They are; **Concealment, Element of Surprise, Distraction,** and **Stealth.**

Another important strategy is choosing the right victim-- the old, weak, sick, defenseless (young) or distracted. And there is also the tactic of separating the intended victim from its envelope of safety or isolating it from the herd to ambush it when the prey is in its least defensible (most vulnerable) position. The lion or tiger will not ever attack the strongest male or female in the herd, thereby risking injury in which case he then becomes the prey. Also important is the fact that he will not attack the intended victim if he has been discovered prior to attacking. This is why all *prey* animals are so alert, have good eyesight, great hearing and use the strategy of posting lookouts that sound the alarm if a predator is discovered.

Now, important in all of this is that the same principles that apply to these wild animals apply to the human animal. The human predator has a job. His job is to get up in the morning, go out and get what he wants from me or you, go to McDonalds, eat, go home and watch T.V. till midnight. He wants to use the least amount of effort (energy) to accomplish his task and he does not want to fight, get injured, caught, seen, or threatened in his efforts. So, back to my original premise that as animals, the same principles apply to us as in the predator/prey relationship in nature. We can analyze, learn, strategize, and prepare ourselves to prevent becoming the prey part of that equation.

As a result of interviewing individuals who spent a majority of their free existence stalking and attacking other human prey, we can devise a strategy and a pre-attack response to remove ourselves from their radar screen. These predators, which include muggers, robbers, rapists, and serial killers, all agree with the following: they pick the easiest, weakest, most vulnerable, unaware, victims and use the tactics of ambush and surprise to accomplish their goals.

In reality, when scanning a crowd for potential victims, they spend only a couple of seconds on each individual as they I.D. potential victims.

In essence it's a scan of *"go—no go"* simplicity in the selection process. Then it is a further sorting of reward value, money, or something else the predator desires. And then a further sorting of situational circumstances: she's drunk, she's alone, or he's flashing a wad of cash and he's unaware. All this takes place in a matter of seconds, because just like an animal in the wild, the human predator is a professional whose continued existence depends on the mastery of his skills.

Those skills are focus and attack, with a singular purpose. You on the other hand are not singularly focused on preventing an attack. In almost all cases, the *last* thing on the minds of victims is that they may be the potential target of an attack. That is why it is so easy and happens so often. It is important to know that there are two main categories of human predators, the Resource Predator and the Process Predator. The Resource Predator is one who attacks for personal gain: money, jewelry, anything that "pays" him for his efforts. The Process Predator is a different creature altogether. His reward is the pain he causes in the victim, the suffering, the domination, the fear, and maybe, the kill.

Now, knowing the strategies of the predator, we are able to consciously strategize, and employ active countermeasures and pre-emptive tactics to the predator's actions to prevent them from coming to fruition. In order to prevent yourself from being seen as a potential victim to predators that you *will* encounter, take heed of the steps listed below:

1. *Darkness is a friend of the predator, not the prey.* Stay in a well-lit area always. In a parking lot, park as close as you can to a street light.

2. *Do not separate from the herd.* Do not go anywhere by yourself, even the bathroom, the parking lot, or anywhere, by yourself. There is safety in numbers.

3. *Be aware.* (Reference "Situational Awareness" in this book) The alert lookout is rarely targeted for attack.

4. *Stand tall.* Carry yourself in a way that radiates confidence and an imposing bearing. F**k with me and you've got a fight on your hands. "Choose someone easier," is the essence of this idea.

5. And finally, *look people in the eye.* There is an old saying among criminals that is still true and relevant. "The only person that looks you in the eye is either a cop or a bad guy." The surest way to pre-empt a possible attack is to I.D. the attacker. And that is by looking him in the eye. This is not a challenge stare, a glare, scowl, or

stare down. It is merely a glance, but an eye to eye glance, that says loud and clear, "I've seen you, and I know you're there. I'm aware of you."

Now, how do you know in a room, a bar, or in any environment just who that bad guy is? You don't. But remember what I said earlier? The only one who will look you in the eye is either a cop or a bad guy? Well, if you catch someone looking at you, return the look. If it's a cop, there's nothing to worry about. If it's a bad guy, you've ID'ed him and he'll move on. When I enter a room, a restaurant, a bar, etc., I scan the room (see situational awareness). I look at everybody in the room and I look at their eyes. I want everyone to know I've seen them and I'm aware of them. I've certainly been in my share of fights, but I haven't been caught off guard and I haven't been attacked--yet.

Chapter 3

Your Gut Never Lies

If there's any doubt, there's no doubt.

Have you ever said to yourself, "I knew I never should have done that?" Or have you reached down to pick up a box thinking maybe I should get someone's help, then just decided, "Oh what the heck, I'll get it," which leads to, "Oh, my back! I knew it. Why did I do that?" So what just happened here? Well, there's always a plethora of interesting factors at play in everything we say or do. But what we are looking at here is somewhat obvious and it is something I can pretty darn well guarantee has happened to all of us. It revolves around one very clear thought and statement that we have all made: "I knew I shouldn't have done that." How did you know? Let's answer that question at least as it pertains to this discussion.

Have you ever heard of the expression, "Your gut feeling?" "I had a gut feeling about that guy," or "My gut was telling me something wasn't right." You can call it what you'd like, intuition, a bad vibe, the hairs on your neck, etc. I'm calling it your *gut feeling*. I'm about to ask you to accept another premise. And here it is: **your gut feeling is never wrong,** ever. I don't have the luxury of time or space to analyze or diagnose exactly what a gut feeling is, but you all know what I'm talking about, because we've all got it. Perhaps it is one part of an evolutionary survival skill that kept us from going extinct along with so many other creatures over the millennia. I don't know if other animals have it to any degree, but I suspect they do. But, I can certainly tell you that one thing they don't have is the power to reason. And that's what gets us into a lot of trouble. It is that element that allows us to talk ourselves out of listening to our gut feel--a primal survival instinct. Stop doing that!

We are all taught not to be rude, not to hurt someone else's feelings, that it's wrong to make someone else feel uncomfortable. I'm not saying that these are bad things, but in the context of a potential threat or danger, then it doesn't matter. Most of the time you're dealing with a stranger you'll never see again, so what does it really matter? Understand that I'm not suggesting that you always need to be rude, get in someone's face, or even be inconsiderate. But just remember, a bad guy (a predator) is always trying to lead you into a trap, using charm, humor, manners, intimidation, fear, trickery, or deceit and you might need to be a rude, inconsiderate bastard if needed, to throw him off your track. Feel free to do so without hesitation. It doesn't really matter what tools the predator uses. Your gut feel, this survival tool, is your best friend. It puts your safety and well-being above all other concerns. It will never lie to you or deceive you. Just shut up and listen to it.

It exists for one purpose and one purpose only: *to keep you safe.* There is no other reason for its existence.

The key is to let your gut feel do its job. There's an old spook maxim that I used at the beginning of this chapter, "If there's any doubt- there's no doubt." That saying has kept a lot of operators alive and it will keep you alive too—if you let it. Like I said earlier, it's our brain that gets in the way, our reason, and our inability to make a decision. If it doesn't feel right to go into that room, don't do it. If it doesn't feel right to walk down the dark sidewalk to your car, don't do it. If there's something that doesn't seem just right about the guy offering you that drink, don't take it. If it doesn't feel right to take that next step, don't do it.

So, anytime that you get a bad feeling about something, there is a reason for it. Your gut instinct is speaking to you. In fact it is shouting at you. But for most of us, it's at a subconscious level. What you need to do is start listening to it. Your internal radar has reached out, looked downrange, and has identified a threat or a potential danger. So listen and take heed. In times when you suspect or *feel* that you are being manipulated, conned, coerced, or cornered into an uncomfortable situation, a simple and definitive **No Thank You** will often take you out of their game plan. If your gut says no, then your mouth should too.

In order for you to get in tune with your inner protection, just like any other skill, you have to practice it. You can start by actively trying to become conscious of what it's trying to tell you. Now you're going to have to sort through a lot of chaff to get to the "real deal feel," but over time it will become evident when your gut feel is talking and what your gut feel is talking about.

The big hurdle is in knowing what your gut is saying, and what you think your gut should be saying. One is real and the other is you thinking about what you think your gut should be telling you. Over time, and given a context of the event that is taking place, you will be able to tell your head from your gut. Remember one may try to lead you astray. The other never will. Sometimes the best choice is not to think, but just to listen.

Chapter 4

The Will to Survive

Second place is last place and in this case, second place is the morgue.

One thing that has proven to be a common factor among almost all survivors of a life or death situation is a constant, conscious, almost overpowering, will to survive. Even when lacking some of the other *Seven Essential Skills*, the will to live has often times been a deciding factor in the outcome. It seems quite obvious to almost everyone that they would of course, want to live. We all want to live, right? Well, I will tell you this. When you are facing death, and I mean actually looking him right in the eye, when there is not one ounce of strength left in your body and you have given everything you have got to give, the thought of giving in, will cross your mind. And in that moment teetering on the brink of giving up or going on, the will to live is likely going to be the one thing that tips the balance in your favor. Some people consciously make the decision to give up, to surrender their will to death's cold embrace. You might say, not me.

Never! I would never do that. I will never give up! Do you really know that for sure?

After dealing with people in high stress environments for most of my adult life, I've seen my share of quitters, and there have been way more than I expected and it has severely disappointed me. Maybe it's my point of view. I don't expect anyone to quit and I certainly have a low tolerance for those that do. I believe that as we become softer as a society, less demanding of high levels of performance, and more concerned with standards of equality rather than stressing competitive excellence, we are creating a society, a culture, a nation of quitters. The problem with that is that once you learn to quit, quitting becomes a habit. It is the easiest thing in the world to do. Why? Because you just do nothing--you quit. Not quitting is the hard part.

Vince Lombardi, legendary coach of the Green Bay Packers once said, "I don't care if a guy gets knocked down. I only care about what he does when he gets up." As a father of three children who all compete in sports, I have seen the culture of competition dissolve into non-contests where there are no points, no winner (we're all winners), and teams where every player gets a trophy, even for finishing in last place. That is so we don't damage anyone's "self-esteem." Yet true self-esteem is actually *built* by facing loss or failure and then deciding, "I don't like to lose. I'm going to try harder next time." That's what builds self-esteem and a no-quit attitude. Vince Lombardi also said, "Show me a good loser and I'll still show you a loser." The question I now ask is how sure are you that you, would *never* quit? Are you a product of the modern values of "equality above excellence?" Well, so far I have said quite a bit about quitting and about what I think may be the contributing factors to a quitter's attitude. So what about not quitting?

Earlier I made the statement that *quitting* becomes a habit. Let me tell you something about habits. Habits don't care if they are good or bad. A habit is a learned behavior.

Why would I ever want to learn something that is not good for me? So it is with quitting. If I can learn to quit, I can damn sure learn to not quit. But there is more. What it consists of is the mental or psychological aspect of never giving up. The mind can be trained just like the body. You must also teach your mind that you are not a quitter, and that you will never give up for any reason ever.

You must drill it into your psyche just as you train your body, through constant and never ending affirmations that you are not a quitter. You have to convince your mind to the point where it becomes a foundation of your being. You have to know, you have to believe, that in the game of life or death, second place is not just second place. It's not just last place--it's the morgue. There is also another aspect to the will to survive that I haven't discussed yet: the reason to live. In wartime combat, many times soldiers have revealed that in the heat of battle they were not fighting for their country, nor were they fighting for themselves. They were fighting to save their teammates, or their buddies. They had a reason to live, a reason to carry on, and to never give up.

How do you learn how to be one who never quits, the one who never gives up? Well the surest way to build this good habit, is to start practicing it. And the best way to do that is to literally push yourself to those quitting moments again and again. Every time you can, push yourself through to carry on, to do a few more reps, another couple of laps, a couple of more rounds. Even better than solo training, is competition. Whether it is running, boxing, swimming, or another competitive endeavor, head to head competition against another human being teaches you a lot about yourself. The lessons are about reaching your limit and through sheer force of will, choosing to push on a little longer, a little farther, a little harder. By doing so you are teaching yourself that you can always do more; that you are never at "the end of your rope." In the same vein, when alone and facing possible death, many survivors have talked about what gave *them* the will to live.

Many times it was faith, faith in God, faith in a cause or an ideal. It could be as basic as wanting to see your wife again, your children, or perhaps to be able to walk your daughter down the aisle at her wedding. It was a reason not to give up and that is what the will to live is all about. So the question I will leave you with is this. Do you have the will, a reason, to live? Only you can answer that question. I hope that when the time comes you have the right answer.

Chapter 5

Fight for Your Life

Make my kids orphans or his kids orphans? That's a no brainer." – Rory Miller

Many of you who are reading this are actively involved in training -training on how to engage another human being in combat. That training could be part of your job, for sport, for fitness, or for self-defense. Your training might be defensive tactics, military combatives, firearms training, MMA, Judo, Jiu-Jitsu, or any combination of martial arts/combative arts training. However, there is a big difference between self-defense training (the way most combat arts are taught) and training to kill another human being who's trying to take your life. Here is the difference. What I need you to understand is in order to perpetuate an attack a predator must always possess at least two attributes. Those two attributes are *means and intent*. Although there are other attributes that are present, without these an attack could not take place.

Now, I'm going to ask you to remember what I've said earlier. Principles do not care where they are applied and they do not know the difference between good or bad. They are just principles and they are always in play and they don't care whose side they are on. So if you accept that premise, then two basic things emerge. By knowing that these principles are universal truths that always apply and that they are always the same, gives me the opportunity to prepare for them. I can develop strategies, tactics, and training that will prepare me to combat and defeat them. The second thing to emerge from the acceptance of this premise is that the same principles that apply to the bad guy also apply to me. And that is where I shall now go.

I've been around combative training my entire life and I've seen every kind of student, every personality type, and individual you could imagine. And I've seen thousands of individuals throughout my career who have come and gone. Very few have made the study of combat preparation a lifelong part of their lives. And that's ok. I would never expect anything different. A lot of us had piano lessons as a child but did not go on to become a professional musician. It's just not everyone's cup of tea. For the ones who continued to pursue tactical/combat training in any of its forms, be it physical combat or firearms training there is one aspect of their training, that is, rarely if ever, addressed.

That is the *difference* between means and intent. There is a phenomenon in Law Enforcement called a "Hesitation Shooting." What is bad about it is that it usually involves a cop getting killed. Imagine this scenario. A police officer is called to a scene and confronts an armed assailant. It may be known to the officer that the bad guy may have already killed someone on scene. The bad guy confronts the officer, points his gun at the officer and has on occasion even stated, "You're going to die." The officer with his own gun drawn and pointed at the suspect just can't believe it when suddenly he feels an impact in his chest like a major league fastball, falls to his back and the world slowly fades to black. What just happened doesn't happen to all cops, just some, and it even happens with soldiers, sometimes even while bad guys are trying to kill them.

Well, there are lots of dynamics in play, but the most important ones are these.

1. One guy was bad--one guy was good.

2. The bad guy has done it before.

3. The bad guy didn't mind killing. The good guy did.

In actuality the police officer had the upper hand--on paper anyway. He had the law on his side. He had the right to shoot to kill and he had the responsibility to do so in the case just described. He had the physical skills and training in using his firearm against a bad guy and he had all the training to know how to deal with scenarios involving dealing with armed suspects. But, what was left out? He lacked the *intent* to kill. He had the means, but not the intent. The bad guy had both the means and the intent. Guess who wins with that hand?

I've seen so many individuals spend hundreds of hours on the mat and thousands of rounds at the range training their physical self to possess the means to do violence, *deadly violence* against another human being. But, how much of that time is spent instructing yourself in the harsh reality of having to take another person's life? We still live in a fairly homogenous society with the shared values of what is commonly called good or bad behavior. We are the product of our value system, as passed to us by our families, our friends, our society, our religion, and our laws, both moral and judicial.

And one of those values is a big one: Thou shalt not kill. That commandment didn't come with an asterisk *unless you need to*. And in the case of that 6th Commandment I really, truly believe, it originally meant thou shall not commit murder, the unjustified taking of another life. The "justified" taking of another life is something I for one have reconciled my beliefs with. So as a whole, we are taught from day one that all life is sacred and that we must not break that covenant with our fellow man. However, there are those of us who must be ready to break that covenant and to break it without hesitation. Now, before anyone gets the idea that I advocate raining down death and destruction on someone who might have just given me the finger on the freeway, let me say this. Deadly force is only employed if it is warranted, justified, and necessary.

Remember, the title of this book, "The Seven Strategies to Survive a *Deadly* Attack." The premise of this book is to prepare you for *that* scenario and remember everything I describe in this book is based on the premise that you are facing a deadly attack. Bruce Lee once said he viewed a violent confrontation like this: "Bruise my skin and I smash into your flesh. Smash into my flesh and I fracture your bones. Fracture my bones and I take your life. Do not be concerned with escaping safely-lay your life before him."

In order to survive a true, deadly attack, you must be willing to pull out all the stops and be willing to do whatever it takes to save yourself or your loved ones. All the training in the world will do you no good in that extreme moment, if you do not have the intent. In the midst of a violent attack, there is only one thing that thwarts the attack-- more violence. And that violence must come from you.

Chapter 6

Loss of Self

Lose yourself to win the fight.

Have you ever seen two boxers staring each other down in the center of the ring before the fight? Why do you think they do this? Simply, they are trying to psychologically intimidate each other. Two simple psychological statements are being made. One is, "I'm not scared of you," and the other is, "I'm going to kick your ass!" This interaction, in easy, seeable, and understandable terms, defines the classic "psyching out your opponent," that we've all heard of at some point in our life.

That example is a very easy way to illustrate the psychological interaction of human behavior between two individuals engaged in or about to engage in combat. However, there's a lot more going on than meets the eye. In real combat the stakes are not whose hand is raised at the end, but who ends up in a coffin.

As I've discussed all along, vital if not primary is the role the mind plays in surviving a life-threatening encounter. Now we'll take a look at what role it plays during combat itself.

The apex predator in North America is the male grizzly bear. It is 800 pounds of tooth, claw, and muscle. It can kill a 700 pound elk with one blow and it fears no other species of animal.

Yet there is one animal that can and will kill a male grizzly. What animal could that be? That animal is a 400 pound female grizzly. How could that possibly be? The male outweighs her by 400 pounds and is bigger, meaner, and stronger. The answer to the question is this: when the female is defending her young. As you know in the wild, males will often kill the offspring sired by other males in order to drive the females into estrus so they can pass on their progeny and genes.

How can the female kill a bear that dwarfs it in size? There are several major dynamics at work and in total, give the female the advantage that she needs. They are that she will fight to kill the male grizzly (Purpose and Intent). She has no regard for her own safety (Loss of

Self). And, she will fight to the death (Ferocious Resolve).

I want to look at these three separate but necessary parts of the whole as they relate to combat and what their effects are on you, their effects on the opponent and why are they necessary for your survival when you are confronted with the harsh realities of a violent encounter?

We'll start with **Purpose** and **Intent.** Using the female grizzly as our model, if she is attacked by a male grizzly over territory, food, or any reason excluding protecting her young, the male grizzly would easily subdue her, drive her away or kill her. Or perhaps he is just a serial killer grizzly and she was to become his latest victim.

What is difference? Same bears, same fight – but no purpose. The difference is plain to see. She didn't have anything to fight for. There was no purpose to fight. She did not want to hurt or kill the male grizzly – no Intent. She could always get other food or move to another territory. So in this case the male grizzly dominates the other bear both physically and psychologically. Just as with humans, who after all are still animals, there *must* be a purpose to fight, a cause, or a reason, or the heart just won't be in it.

This purpose, whether it is to protect children, loved ones, partners, teammates, or the soldier next to you is a vital element of survival against the odds. This purpose can also be driven by less tangible but sometimes just as important reasons such as religion, justice, patriotism or moral righteousness. Sometimes it's just plain self-preservation. Whatever that reason is, there *must* be a reason.

In regard to *Intent*, there must be a goal. And that goal must be to meet force of violence by responding with *Overwhelming Force of Violence*. If you must fight you have to fight to win, from the very onset. For example whenever I've worked with the Brits, they were always talking about the switch. Are you switched on? Switch on – switch off – developing your switch, etc.

I came to realize that what they meant was, in simple terms of a fight, your switch better be turned on or you're going to lose. Switched on can also mean being aware of your surroundings, your environment and many other things. If you enter into the fight, any fight without the

Intent to Kill if necessary, then you may not get that option after you've been stabbed several times, shot or beaten with a pipe. Here's where most attorney types and a lot of Law Enforcement people say, "Hey, wait a minute. You can't tell people to go out and kill someone just because that person said, "F**k you, I'm gonna kick your ass!" So let me just say this once again, the premise of this book is; "Surviving the **Deadly** Attack."

The female grizzly enters the fight to protect her young at full blood lust rage knowing that if she has to, she will kill the male grizzly, she doesn't *ramp up* to fight the male bear during the attack. Perhaps a more benign analogy follows; just picture this and you'll know the difference I'm describing. Walk over to your stereo and turn it on. Now adjust the volume. Turn it up so you can hear it where you want it to be.

Or walk over to the stereo turn the volume up to full blast and then hit the on switch. That is the difference I am talking about. Against true, raw, naked violence you don't have the option of turning up the volume, or "ramping up" to fight off an attacker *during* the attack. You need to hit him at full volume and then turn the volume down as is warranted both morally and legally as the dynamics change. You've got to switch on at full volume until the threat is neutralized. Sometimes just "putting up your dukes," stops a fight before it starts as long as you are ready to go "all the way." If that is your intent, the opponent will get the message – psychologically. It speaks loud and clear without a word being said.

The second aspect of the fight between the minds is this. The Japanese Samurai called it **"The loss of self."** What this means is that in order to fight, really fight with everything that you have, with no hesitation or holding back, you can have no regard for injury or harm to yourself. Why was this important to the Samurai? Because when two opponents are fighting each other in mortal combat with razor sharp swords that will cut a man in half, there can be no hesitation, second guessing or fear of being cut or injured. "He who hesitates is lost," is absolutely true in terms of mortal combat. Many times we have been regaled with stories of soldiers who fought the enemy against incredible odds, with serious injuries, that would be enough to disable someone under "normal" conditions.

If you've ever had the opportunity to hear or talk to any of those individuals, you will find that they had "ceased to exist" in those moments and that there was only the enemy; that everything in their being was channeled to defeating or killing the enemy. There was nothing held back. It was pure focus and determination at the cost of all other considerations. There was NO FEAR! Mind you, I'm not talking about courage here. Although that is also something that is certainly necessary in combat. And many times that courage is fueled by purpose as we discussed earlier.

However, what I'm talking about here is a state of mind, a psychological phenomenon. It is also part of what enables the grandmother to pick the car up, off her grandson. There is no, "I can't pick up the car." There is no, "It's too heavy for me." There is no *I* or *me*. There is only, "PICK UP THE CAR!" I call this the Superman moment. We all have it. You may have never used it, but you've got to believe it exists.

The third and very vital component of the battle of the wills is *I will fight to the death,* **Ferocious Resolve.** When the female grizzly is defending her young she will fight to the death to protect them, willfully sacrificing herself to save her babies. This is the never give up – never surrender state of being that gives you the resolve and the ferociousness of a cornered deadly animal. Somehow the male grizzly knows this and it has an effect. It's not visible, it's not physical, but it's felt. The male grizzly feels it and it gives the female a huge psychological advantage over the male.

The knowledge that you will fight to the death is a powerful potion. Most people will never know if they would or if they could. I guess what that proves is that our laws, our system, and our individual morals and ethics are in good working order, which is a good thing.

However there are people – very bad people in our midst- -that intend to do us harm, and given the right circumstances will perpetrate their evil deed. You might be one whose path is never crossed by such evil and if so, consider yourself lucky.

But for the Warrior, who sees danger where others are oblivious, there is no doubt about the question: Will I fight to the death? He already knows the answer.

In a conventional confrontation, in the brief seconds prior to the first strike or blow, the battle of the minds has already begun and the battle of the wills is already engaged. In the case of a surprise attack or ambush, the battle of the minds begins simultaneous to the physical engagement, but it is still taking place throughout the encounter.

In any case, if all other things are equal, (size, strength, and skill) then the combatant with the psychological edge will usually win the battle. In a lot of cases where the opponent has the edge in strength, size, and skills, the combatant with the strongest resolve, the greatest force of will still win the fight even against the odds.

If your opponent senses that he is up against a true Warrior, one who is projecting the following: I'm fighting for a righteous purpose. I'll kill you if I have to. I don't care what happens to me and I will fight to the death, then your opponent knows immediately the price he is about to pay for his mistake. And the moment he senses that, and knows that he is up against a 10 foot tall, fire-breathing dragon, his resolve will crumble and the warrior will prevail.

In so many cases the battle of the minds determines the outcome of the battle of the fists. You must be armed and prepared to fight on both fronts to be the winner. Just remember never to neglect one, for the other.

Chapter 7

Never do Anything Without a Purpose

Never do Anything that is Useless

When it comes to a battle for survival in a life or death struggle, it is imperative and vital that you only act with a purpose. You never do anything unless it is necessary to further your chances of survival. The title of this chapter is actually two sides of the same coin, and one cannot exist without the other, especially in the context of hand-to-hand combat.

Unfortunately so much of what we are taught in schools, martial arts training, and various self-defense courses, has no purpose and it is useless. That is because most of these schools of training are banking on one thing first and foremost, and that is cash flow. After all, it's how they make their living. And cash flow only exists if there are students in the class. So teaching or even talking about the brutal realities of fighting to the death are avoided because it is not something most people want to hear about, let alone confront or learn about. I've got that. Since most people train for either sport competition or recreation, self-defense as it is taught is a very sanitized and politically correct version of combat. Anything else and most instructors would have an empty school.

However, I've never trained for sport competition or recreation. I've trained for one reason and one reason only--to fight, and to fight to the death if necessary. As a result of over forty years of serious training and teaching, I did find that there were others like myself, mostly military or former military along with a handful of civilians. As a result of training and interacting within *this* circle, it became evident that certain things were held in common and they were always present in the way things were analyzed, taught and used. Two of the most important tenets were simple but profound;

Never Do Anything Without a Purpose

Never Do Anything That Is Useless.

How do these statements apply to hand-to-hand combat? Why are they so important? Here is a fact. No matter how prepared you are for combat, or how well you are trained, luck is always part of the equation. Mike Tyson once said, "Everybody's got a plan until the first guy gets hit in the teeth." In other words, you can't control what another human being is going to do and most of the time you can't predict their actions either. Any boxer will tell you that a lucky shot will knock you out just the same as a well- set-up right cross.

And in a fight, the longer a fight lasts, the more luck enters into the equation. In other words the longer the fight lasts, the greater the odds that your opponent may get in that lucky shot. And if it's with a weapon, knife or gun, the results are disastrous. You want to end the fight quickly and decisively or you may want to fight only long enough to get away. Either way the goal is to not prolong the fight.

Two of the statements that I use in my classes are these: ***Economy of Motion--Efficiency of Action*** which are equally as important as the two statements at the beginning of this chapter.

Everything that I teach and everything you learn and practice should embody and physically express those two ideals. If they don't, then I'm not doing my job. If they don't apply to what you may be learning from any instructor, then he's not doing *his* job.

The key to efficient, effective combat skills is to strip everything away to the bare essentials. The key word in that statement is *essentials*. It means only that which is necessary. Anything else is useless, anything else is unnecessary. So why do it? Why learn it? Why spend anytime practicing it? You can also relate to another statement I use in classes: "An expert is one who has mastered the basics."

Basics are always simple, straight forward, and effective. In the chaos of combat they are the only things that work. So you need to look at your own training and start to strip away anything that you don't absolutely need to use, and further, anything you can't do easily and effectively. You need to be focused like a laser beam on one thing and one thing only; the removal of the threat, the thing that is trying to do you harm. Anything else in that moment is useless unless it is part of the process of destroying that threat effectively, quickly and completely. Why would you do anything else?

Conclusion

It is vitally important to note that having put all of these skills in front of you does not make them happen. You must practice them, all of them. Just like any other skill, the learning process is one thing, the mastering process is another. To master any skill, the key component is practice, practice, and practice. Always remember and be aware of this. People make the judgment of others that they have "natural" talent or that their expertise was easy for them because they were "gifted."

Well the truth is, having been a professional athlete, and knowing many others who were the best in their field, including Hall of Fame members in both Professional Football and Professional Baseball, the real reason they got to their level of skill was because of practice. And I mean *real* practice--long hard grueling hours of it. Long after everyone had gone home, on Saturdays, Sundays, before school, after work, they practiced, they trained and they sacrificed.

They spent hours alone, practicing their craft, their skills, and the fundamentals that they built a career upon. Believe me when I tell you that everything they accomplished was well deserved. No one got there because of natural talents or because they were gifted. They got to the top because they listened, they learned, and they were inspired, enough to separate themselves from all the halfhearted, the quitters, and especially those who were looking for an easy way to the top.

An Air Force Survival instructor once told me, the key to surviving in a life or death environment lies in the ability to make decisions, the right decisions every time and quickly. This sounds daunting and it may appear so to the uninitiated, but it is the reason we have survival schools and it is the reason it is taught to the military. In an emergency, in the gravest extreme, that moment where your survival hangs in the balance, those soldiers or airmen will make the right decision automatically because they have learned and practiced making the right decision before they are forced to, in a real life or death situation.

I have laid out a set of seven essential skills needed to survive a deadly attack. Do you need to apply all seven every time? Sometimes. Sometimes even just one or two will tip the scales in your favor.

But if you are caught unaware, with your guard down with nothing to respond with, you could be facing the last moments of life on earth. It is my hope that no matter what the level of your skill training, that you buttress its effectiveness with the seven essential skills that we have discussed in the course of this book. For those of a non-violent nature who may be reading this, I sometimes admire your kinder, gentler, disposition and the solace it may provide you. But then I awaken from my fantasy and am reminded of the quote attributed to George Orwell, "People sleep soundly in their beds at night because rough men stand ready to do violence on their behalf."

I'd like you to consider the following brief questions. Are you prepared to gouge someone's eyes out? Will you tear his throat out with your teeth? Will you smell his stale breath as his eyes glaze over from your arm around his throat? If you're not willing to answer "yes, *Hell yes*" to those questions, then the day that you meet a real bad guy is the day you are going to die.

I'll put it in terms that maybe more of us can relate to. As fellow trainer, Rory Miller says so clearly, 'Am I am going to let him make my kids orphans? Or am I going to make his kids orphans?" You already know my answer. Do you know what your answer will be?

The consolation in all of this is that, any skill can be taught. I've done my job, now it's your turn.

Good Luck and God Speed.

Ernest Emerson

Bonus Chapter

Thank you for reading this book. I have included as a bonus for you, the first chapter of one of my other books for you to read. If you are interested you can find this book along with all my others to purchase at book stores and online retailers worldwide or for an autographed copy, you can order directly off of the website, TheGuardianShepherd.com

Bonus Articles

As an extra bonus I've also included here two articles from my website TheGuardianShepherd.com, where you will find dozens of free articles and information concerning counter-terrorist training and tactics, personal security, personal family safety, training, conditioning, and self defense. You will also be able to download lectures, seminars and training routines to give you the tools, skills and mentality needed to be the most effective "Guardian Shepherd" for yourself, your family, your loved ones, and others who might need your protection in a time of need.

BONUS CHAPTER

from

The Seven Strategies of Hand To Hand Combat

Chapter 1.

The Strategy of Strategies

Techniques Without Strategy Are Useless

Every plan must have a strategy, otherwise you would never know what you want to do, where you want to do it, or when you wanted to start or stop. How would you ever accomplish anything, if you didn't know what you wanted to do in the first place? Not having a strategy is like taking your car on the freeway and just traveling about aimlessly only changing lanes or taking a turn when the other drivers forced you to do so. You would be in a completely reactive state, without a choice, only doing things or taking any action when others force you to do so, without a choice. If you are in this type of reactive state in combat you will lose and you will die. Granted this is an extreme analogy because most people when attacked will attempt to defend themselves in some primal way. But to make that "way" more effective, to make it the most effective that it can be, you need a strategy with which you are able to construct a plan. Then you can devise the tactics and/or techniques necessary to carry out the strategy. I believe it was Von Clausewitz who made the simple statement, "Tactics without strategy are useless." It has also been said "All other things being equal, the side with the best strategies will always win." That's my quote and I've found it to be true in all competitions from football to hide and go seek.

Knowing that *"all strategies flow from plans"* and *"tactics flow from strategies,"* it becomes evident that even in our day-to-day activities running around " like a chicken with its head cut off" doesn't do you much good at all. When you are overwhelmed by events or a situation, just stopping, assessing your situation and coming up with a strategy to fix the problem or better your situation, can bring a sense of control, and give you what you need to take care of that situation. Of course, you need to stick to your strategy, especially if it's a sound one. That's the purpose of this book, to give you seven sound battle proven strategies (and a few more tips) for surviving mortal combat against another human being. These seven strategies really define two important statements you'll find in several places throughout this book "Never do anything that is useless." "Never do anything without a purpose." I firmly believe these statements to be true in life-and-death combat, for without a strategy, a game plan, how would I ever know what is useful or useless and how would I ever know if what I was doing served the right purpose toward my goal?

I would like you to imagine something. Imagine a football game where two teams are playing each other. One of the teams, Team 1, is coached by the legendary football coach, Vince Lombardi, whose team has all the skills, tactics and benefits of the master strategist, with a game plan to emphasize his own team strengths while exploiting the weaknesses of the other team. Team 2 is a highly skilled team of players who can run, pass, block, and tackle, equally as well as Vince Lombardi's Team 1. However, they have no coach, no plays to execute, no game plan–no strategy to win. The players on both sides are of the same skill level, the same size and fitness. Which team do you think will dominate the game? Which team do you think will win? Did you pick Team 1, Vincent

Lombardi's team? I hope so. Because then you already know and understand that a game plan or a strategy, can tip the scales in your favor, especially if your strategies are better than your opponent's and most always if your opponent has no strategy at all.

In order to create efficient, effective, and positive results in respect to hand-to-hand combat, you need a strategy for each and all of the separate parts that make up the whole. Of course, the whole or overall umbrella goal is that you survive. That goes without saying.

But, wanting to win is not a strategy.

You need to be able to identify and then break combat down into its essential raw ingredients, its basic parts so that you can then address each of those components individually. By strengthening them, improving them, and tuning them, when they are reassembled you have a stronger whole and the result is that you've created for yourself a better, more effective warrior.

This training of component parts must require that each and all individual components be driven by its own strategy to achieve your desired outcome. Strategy must be the overriding guide for all of your training so that even in practice, you are never doing anything that is useless and never doing anything without a purpose. Let's leave doing things of no use and doing things of no purpose to the bad guys, and hope that those traits become their habits and not ours. (Let's also hope that they don't read this book.)

By defining and applying the strategies in this book, you will start to see where you need improvements and ways you can train to bring about the desired results. Strategists as a rule are not lazy types. It is in their very nature to be more efficient, to not waste time and to try to get as much done as possible in a minimum amount of time. As you progress through this learning process, you will start to see that having a strategy, the right strategy, can be applied to almost everything you do on a daily basis. Once you've made it a habit you will find yourself applying it to more and more of the things that you do. Just don't fall prey to self-doubt. This habit of strategies is not greedy, it's not obsessive, and it's not a waste of time. It's about being efficient in your life and working hard to bring about the positive results you desire, without wasting the precious personal time we are given to exist on this earth. It is extremely important when it comes to training because we already have little time available for friends, family, jobs, and just plain fun. Knowing that I have to train, I want my training time to be as efficient as possible and to produce the best possible results that I can get from the precious time I spend doing so. The strategy of having a strategy will get you from here to there, quick, fast and in a hurry.

BONUS ARTICLE 1 of 2
Force on Force 1

I was recently tasked with creating a training program for a new government agency. Working within such an environment forced me to take a different look at designing a program and curriculum that could be taught by any training instructor to students (recruits) who were complete novices to martial combat/defensive tactics. In other words it had to be a program that was repeatable and teachable, so that anyone enrolled in the program gets a known quantity of skills and any individual who inherits the duties of instructor can without prior experience produce the same results. Basically, pick up the manual and start teaching.

It doesn't sound too complicated at first but taking a lifetime of learning, practicing and teaching and distilling it down to a body of information suited to their needs was quite a daunting task.

It forced me to re-evaluate, quantify and qualify everything that I teach and it gave me some new insights that I will share with you. It has relevance to any form of martial study and can work for hobby martial arts, sport martial arts or combat martial arts. The principles are valid for novice practitioners, intermediate students and professional martial artists including teachers.

Now most instructors teach their methods and systems based on some type of curriculum generally passed to them by their instructors or system, but it is always the case that every instructor adds his own insights, discoveries, personality traits, and physical abilities to that environment. However, if you were told you were going to be gone the day after tomorrow what would you spend the next 48 hours writing down to pass on to your students? I will describe briefly what I did in terms of this program but you can plug in your own needs, wants and goals.

The first thing needed was to identify the required results. What skills did these students need to walk away with? In my case the result was the ability to subdue an attacker armed with a weapon of some type, probably an edged weapon but possibly a firearm. In this case survivability of the student was not the primary concern, preventing the bad guy from accomplishing his goal was needless to say the priority. Identifying the goals and the environment they were to be used in specified what was included and eliminated things that would not apply.

Next, who are the students? Were they young, old, male, female? Were they in shape athletes or middle aged professionals taking on a new job assignment? Luckily for me these were all young men, and women who were in top physical shape. Knowing who the students are helped me refine how and what would be going into the program and what physical level of activity we would be training at.

There were other factors that came into play such as how much training time was to be allotted, what level of experience did the students possess, what weapons would be available to them and even such things as their mode of dress.

After identifying these parameters the next important aspect was identifying the principles, concepts and techniques that would be taught. What was I going to teach and how was I going to teach it? Most important of all, would it work? This element brought out something that was absolutely crucial to the success of the curriculum. Would it work for the average man? Here is something that all instructors have to be acutely aware of. It is not whether the techniques will work for you but whether they will work for someone else. If I was 6'4" tall and weighed 245 lbs I could get away with a lot more techniques than if I was 5'7" tall and weighed 145 lbs. What works for you might never work for the average man. The average man in this case was 5'9" tall and 165 lbs, exceptional level of fitness, extremely motivated with an already highly developed warrior ethos. But, no previous hand-to-hand combat experience.

In order to insure that I was going to cover all of my requirements and theirs, I had to categorize the training into three main categories so that I could be sure that everything meshed and no deficits were left open.

Here is a brief synopsis of the three categories needed to codify the training.

1. Hard Skills Training

    This is the nuts and bolts training phase. This is a punch. This is a kick. In firearms training this is the initial phase where you would teach gun safety, function of the weapon, sight alignment, trigger press, etc. In other words, the basics. This is where I cover, how to punch, how to kick (we used two kicks – a foot stomp and a front stomp kick) stance, footwork and body mechanics. There is obviously much more including takedowns various strikes and locks, etc. But all had to be quick, effective and efficient in a gross motor skills environment.

2. Soft Skills Training

In essence this is, when to punch, when to kick. Where to punch. Where to kick. When to take down etc. Now would be where we are starting to apply these skills against an opponent under more dynamic conditions. At this point the student needs to learn to work for his techniques against an ever increasing non-compliant opponent eventually leading up to an opponent who is progressing from merely non-compliant to active, aggressive actions. In shooting this would equate to, shooting from various positions, behind cover, on the move, low light, and multiple targets, moving targets and good guy/bad guy targeting. The introduction to (shoot no shoot training). This is where you apply the mechanics of dynamics environments. This also equates in terms of a sports analogy you are trying your plays in a scrimmage against an opposing team, its close but it is not for real yet. If something doesn't work you get to try again.

3. Active Mental Training

After you have acquired the Hard Skills and are familiar with their use and applications, it really boils down to decision making under stress. I have always stated the following in every class I have ever taught. "You never want to experience something for the first time – in combat." This is the phase where you practice your skills in as close to the actual environment, where they will be used as possible. In terms of firearms training this is usually called Force-on-Force. If you were a member of an assault team this is when you would practice dynamic room entry and hostage rescue against live opponents who are shooting back (simulations or air soft weapons). In this kind of training, high stress, noise, spontaneous actions of the opponents and fear, you will begin immediately to see the difference between what you can do and what you want to do. It may be a wide gap at first but it narrows considerably as you practice under these realistic conditions. Mistakes will be made. But, this is where you want those mistakes to be made. This is where you get the do-over until you get it wired.

In terms of martial arts training for whatever your purpose, at least some aspect of your training should reflect the conditions (as real as possible) for the arena where you will use these skills.

It is important that you realize these three phases of training are not separate or segregated from each other. They overlap, overlay and sometimes occur simultaneously in training. But, for the purpose of discussing them here they appear separate. In reality they are not.

Be it sport, hobby or combat, these three phases of training apply across the board. Just take the aspects that can benefit your end goals and apply them as you need. It is important though to know, really know that you only get out of your training what you are willing to put into it. My training motto is: Train like a Madman... Fight like a demon.

-Ernest R. Emerson

BONUS ARTICLE 2 of 2

Against the Gun

To Fight or Not To Fight

One question that always comes up whenever we get ready to teach gun disarms is, "Can I get shot?" The answer is yes. The next question that comes up then is, "Why would I do something that could get me shot?" The answer to this is, if you know someone is going to shoot you, do you want to just stand there and let him put a bullet right through your heart? The next question is, "How do I know when someone is going to shoot me?" My answer is; I don't know.

Every single situation is different and unique. The dynamics of every armed encounter carry with them a unique set of circumstances. Some of these are the circumstances leading up to the encounter, the state of mind of the attacker, the personality of the attacker, the purpose of the attack, the events taking place around and during the attack, and your reaction to the attack. These are just some of the most obvious. There are a myriad of other complexities that are involved and each one adds to your reaction, "your gut feel" and ultimately your decision to take action or not. For example, if a bad guy shoots the guy standing next to you and then points the gun at you, there is a high probability you're going to get shot. You're going to need to do something.

Before I go any further, let me briefly touch on one point. Very few people are ready for the extreme level of physical violence that is perpetrated during a violent armed attack. This is a good thing for all of us in general. But this is a bad thing if it happens to you. The bad guy uses it to his advantage, knowing from experience that most people go into a state of denial, shock or a sort of mind numbness when confronted with extreme physical violence, whether to themselves or someone in close proximity to them. I'm not going to go into all of the psychological and physiological details as to why, but suffice it to say that many people end up like the "deer in the headlights." That's not what you want to have happen to you.

The bottom line is simply this: if you are confronted with a gun-wielding attacker, you are going to have to make a decision. That decision is going to be based on your overall "take" of the situation and all of the dynamics involved. No one can ever tell you what to do in any of these situations since no two are ever alike. It will be your decision and yours alone if it ever comes down to this moment.

But if you do make the decision to act, what are some of the options that you have available. Bear in mind though, that yes, you can still get shot. However, if I believe that a bad guy is going to shoot me, or one of my loved ones, then I'm going to act. Perfect techniques are only perfect in training. In reality things are always a little bit off, out of balance or harder to execute. But if you follow the principles of the technique and act decisively, you should be able to make it work. The main thing especially when dealing with a gun disarming technique is that if it doesn't work at first, you cannot stop trying. Once you have grabbed the gun, you cannot let go.

Since there are many different scenarios that can manifest in a confrontation against a gun, we'll just discuss several of the more statistically common situations that you may face. In addition these techniques are chosen because they best illustrate the principles that may be applied to most other similar positions that you may encounter.

Beware of a couple of extremely important points.

The first point is this:

The gun will probably fire during the disarm. Due to a reflexive reaction by the bad guy, his finger will probably pull the trigger. That is why it is so important to angle, (move) out of the line of fire while also pushing the gun away from your body. However, in the case of a semi-auto pistol, (not a revolver), by grabbing the barrel and slide during the discharge of the gun, you will prevent the pistol from cycling. This will prevent the casing from ejecting and chambering the next round, effectively jamming the gun. This is why you must perform the tap and rack, when and if you wrest the gun away from the bad guy. Remember, you want to be able to fire the gun if you have to.

The second and perhaps the most important point is:

Getting shot does not mean you are going to die. Statistically, a rather small percentage of people shot with pistols actually die. FBI statistics prove that you are far more likely to die if you are stabbed with a knife than if you are shot. If you are wounded, you can still fight and you can still win. You must be aware of this because most people, as a result of being conditioned by movies and T.V., are likely to "give up" assuming that all gunshot wounds are fatal. **This is not the case.** In the end you are going to be in a fight for your survival and once this struggle has begun, you have to fight as ferociously and as ruthlessly as you can, until you are no longer in danger. In a life or death struggle, your will to live will be as valuable a tool as any of the fighting skills you possess.

There are many disarming techniques that you can use and hopefully if you will experiment with them and apply the principles that I've discussed, you'll discover that there are many more that you can develop and you will find out what works and what does not.

So, in conclusion, even though being faced with a gun may appear to be a no-win situation, it is not. You still have options, many more than you may realize. We all hope never to have to use these skills, but if you ever have to, you'll be thankful to have them in your arsenal.

-Ernest R. Emerson

Recommended Reading List for increasing your ability to Detect, Deny and Destroy

Recommended Reading

The Gift of Fear by Gavin De Becker

On Combat by Lt. Col. David Grossman

On Killing by Lt. Col. David Grossman

Defensive Living by Ed Lovette and Dave Spaulding

Under and Alone by William "Billy" Queen

Terror at Beslan by John Giduck

The Mighty Atom by Ed Spielman

Fearless – Adam Brown by Eric Blehm

The Unthinkable By Amanda Ripley

OTHER BOOKS BY ERNEST EMERSON

Chain Reaction Training

Don't buy this book if you are a quitter. It's not for you. You'll hate it, you'll dismiss it, and you won't see any results. If you're a quitter get out of here. Go to the yoga section.

This is a book about hardcore physical training. It's about functional, combat strength and conditioning. It's not about losing weight or bodybuilding. It's about Warrior Strength.

A warrior needs functional strength. A warrior needs Neanderthal strength, Cro-Magnon Strength, the strength that kept our ancestors alive when everything that existed in their world conspired to kill them, and only the strong survived.

A warrior needs the strength that he can use to fight in combat, survive in combat, or save a teammate in combat. In terms of training, that's a whole different creature than a gym membership workout, a bodybuilding workout, or even what most would consider a *hard* training routine.

Think about it like this. What if you need to sprint a quarter-mile over uneven terrain to rescue a teammate out of a downed Helo, sling him over your back and then carry him back a quarter-mile to a safe position. If you run out of gas or God forbid quit, then your buddy dies. You never want to be that guy. If you follow the Chain Reaction Training protocol you won't.

Developed by Black Belt Hall of Famer and renowned tactical instructor Ernest Emerson, the Chain Reaction System is designed to build 100% usable, all-terrain, combat fitness and strength. Drawing on a lifetime of hands-on experience and knowledge, Emerson is interested in one thing only, optimal human performance.

Just like in his combat classes, Emerson is concerned with getting students to perform at their true maximum potential, far beyond what they may think is the limit of their ultimate efforts.

That is what is needed to survive, and prevail in combat. Life-and-death, hand to hand, combat consists of three fundamental components.

1. The skills

2. The mindset

3. Physical strength and conditioning

All three of these have to be optimized in order to engage in combat with the confidence that you will win. And you know, confidence in combat is a huge factor. Without it you are guaranteed to lose.

There's nothing that builds self-confidence to the degree that being strong and fit does. However, few outside of the Special Operations community, Naval Special Warfare (SEALs), or Olympic athletes ever experience the extreme fitness levels that these 1%ers do.

A friend once asked, "Who do you think is the toughest S.O.B. on earth?" The answer? A 135 pound Marine, just out of boot camp. He is the strongest he has ever been. He is in the best condition he's ever been in, and he knows that in a fight, there's no other human being on earth that will run him out of gas. That is confidence.

The Chain Reaction System is a training regimen that will build that extreme level of fitness and, that extreme level of confidence.

Based on a combination of functional strength, and core conditioning exercises, they are pushed to the extreme by completing a chain from start to finish without stopping. It pushes all three components of physical conditioning, the ATP system, the glycolic system, and the aerobic system to new limits. Limits beyond what you once thought you were capable of doing.

Emerson explains in precise, simple, terms how the system works, why the system works, and then gives you a plan for setting up your own regimen, depending on what equipment or facilities you have available. It leaves you with no excuse for not being able to train. In fact, he provides you 25 days of Chain Reaction Routines, his own routines, which amounts to over a month's worth of training. So if you don't get the results promised, it will only be because of your own weak will and lack of resolve. Emerson leaves you with no excuse.

It has been said that the greatest fear of growing old is that other men stop seeing you as being dangerous. The Chain Reaction Training System will keep you very dangerous. Available at: Emersonknives.com

Surviving Inside The Kill Zone

This is not a book of techniques. This is a book about what you need to know in order to make any technique work when a real bad guy is trying to kill you. Ernest Emerson is an instructor, author and lecturer. He is a Black Belt Hall of Fame member, owner of the Black Shamrock Combat Academy and one of the most sought after tactical instructors in the world. One of his most popular lectures, is titled "Surviving Inside the Kill Zone." He has often been asked the question, "When are you going to put this in a book?" That question is now answered.

This book not only covers all the material of the lecture/seminar but much more than can be discussed in a two hour classroom lecture.

In the brutal arena of life and death combat, there are things that you can do and things you can't. There are also things you should always do and there are things you should never do. And the right things that you are able to do in combat are the ones that will enable you to survive a deadly attack.

Emerson always starts this lecture with the question; "How many first responders are in this room?" There are always several police, firemen, or paramedics in the audience who raise their hands. And then the lecture starts.

In this book you will learn the principles, concepts, strategies, and tactics behind the training methods Ernest Emerson has been teaching to members of Special Operations Units, Government Agencies, and Counterterrorist Units for over two decades.

The book breaks down the subject into seven related but distinct chapters that starts with Education, stressing the importance of learning strategies, tactics, weapons, and methodologies of the bad guys.

Emerson then follows with a further exploration and recommendation for choosing the right weapons, how to judge a training system, and how to identify what you really need to know and how to learn it.

Emerson explains why half of what you know, won't work in combat and only about half of what really works in combat is what you'll actually be able to do. That only leaves about 25% combat effectiveness, when you're up against someone is who trying to take your life. This book gives you the tools to make that 25% more effective and powerful than the other 75% left behind.

The book introduces you to the rules of combat, the important role of goals, the right strategic objectives, and how to apply them to both training and combat. Emerson provides valuable insight into the predator/prey relationship and how you can use it to work against a predator to effectively take you off their, "radar" as a potential prey. Learn how to identify and break the sequence of events that leads to a surprise attack.

Mr. Emerson also teaches the CIA maxim of Detect, Deny, Destroy, and explains how a system that works so well for their officers can be used to work just as well for you.

Knowing that the physical battle is only part of any aggressive or violent confrontation, Emerson devotes an entire chapter to the Warrior Mindset and also the importance of the Will in developing the absolute conviction that you will never quit and never, ever give up, using the same techniques as taught to U.S. Navy SEALs. There is also very valuable information on developing the Mental Trigger, material that until now has never been covered in any other civilian source.

And you will learn how functional conditioning and strength play a vital role in your ability to fight and prevail against the attacker. Combat strength and conditioning is explained in terms that allow you to reevaluate your training regimen and fine tune it for optimum combat performance.

It was mentioned that at the beginning of his lecture, "Surviving Inside the Kill Zone" he asks how many first responders are in the room? Emerson asks the same question at the end of the lecture. This time every hand in the room goes up. Read this book and get ready to raise your hand.

Get your copy at:

Emersonknives.com or TheGuardianShepherd.com

The 7 Strategies of Hand-To-Hand Combat

Black Belt Hall of Famer and Tier One tactical instructor, Ernest Emerson opens the doors to once hidden Strategies, Tactics, and Mentality of the world's deadliest warriors, giving you the tools to upgrade your training in any system, into a truly effective program of combat ready skills.

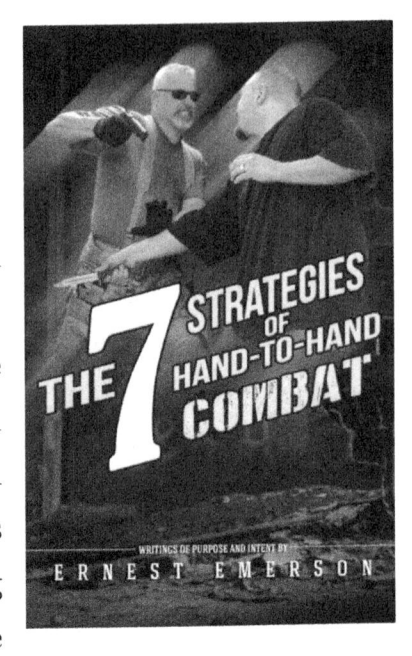

Emerson's genius is in being able to break down human conflict (combat) into its most basic component parts and then explain them in terms that make perfect sense. Then in turn, he gives you the ability to train and supercharge those components individually so that when they are reassembled the result is an Abrams tank powered by jet engines.

But you must be cautioned, if you're looking for a book on how to block a punch, you won't find it here. This is not a book of techniques. This is about giving you the means to create a supercharged capability to take what you already know to the elite level, ready for actual combat.

The difference between Tier One operators and the rest of us is not that they know more techniques or possess secret skills. They know the same things as we do. They just know how to do them much better. Emerson takes you into his classroom to teach you the real secrets, the forbidden knowledge of the warrior elite, America's Special Operations and Black Ops Units.

The problem with training for real-world hand-to-hand combat skills is that almost all martial arts are over 200 years removed from actual combat and have been softened up or "sporterized" to be palatable to the general public. The difference between conventional training and combatives training is defined by two simple words; intent and intensity. Each needs the other to be maximally effective and conventional martial arts lack both.

Without truly knowing if something will actually work in live combat, how can an instructor teach combat skills to someone whose life may depend on those skills?

If you are ever in a situation where you're face-to-face with pure evil, one who is hell-bent on your destruction, and you're not both physically and mentally prepared for violent, deadly, combat, then that is the day you will likely die.

The author shows that you must be able to bring violence of action against the bad guy to such a degree that it doesn't just counter his attack, but destroys him, for attempting to do you harm.

You will learn how to evaluate your current training against the criteria of the perfect technique, to judge everything you do as to whether it will work in real combat or not, and avoid wasting your valuable time doing things that are of no value.

Learning and applying principles and concepts outlined in this book will give you the confidence you need, to never ever wonder again, "Will this really work, or can I do this?" You will learn that the true mastery of fighting skills is not just based on confidence in the techniques, but ultimately in the confidence you have in yourself.

Some of the subjects covered in detail include;

1. The principles, strategies, and tactics, of combat.

2. The physical, physiological, and psychological effects of combat on the human body and how to use them to your advantage.

3. The Three Laws of Combat and the Six Instinctual Triggers.

4. The high art of preemptive self-defense.

5. The importance of being able to distinguish between capability and capacity.

Combative fighting skills, is not a martial art. It is hard, intense, painful training along with the development of the Warrior Mindset, which is really more valuable than any other skill you possess. Without that mindset and the iron will to win, you are only using half of your power. The other half is in the mind. You will learn how important it is to never neglect one for the other.

Ernest Emerson has worked with members of the Naval Special Warfare Community, Navy SEALs, for over 25 years. He carried a DOD top secret clearance for 15 years. He is the owner of Emerson Knives, Incorporated and the Black Shamrock Combat Academy in Los Angeles California.

Get your copy at:

Emersonknives.com or TheGuardianShepherd.com

VIDEOS BY ERNEST EMERSON
Unconventional Edged Weapons Combat I-V

This instructional series is the educational equivalent of a master's degree in Edged Weapons Combat. This is a course. It is a series of instructional evolutions enabling you to super charge your fighting skills. Taught in a progressive layering system using the Accelerated Learning Protocol this course takes you, (regardless of your previous experience or expertise) to a new level of dynamic and unprecedented skill in Edged Weapons Combat. This material has never been available to anyone outside of personal instruction by Ernest Emerson who is regarded as one of the world's leading instructors to military and government agencies worldwide.

VOLUME I
FOUNDATIONS

Building a solid foundation is the fundamental core of developing the Ultimate Fighter. This volume contains the principles and drills needed to develop efficient movement, combat footwork, regaining your stance from the ground and development of the Universal Fighting Stance. Drills and techniques for accessing and deploying your knife are covered, as well as a Bonus Track - Warm up and Stretch.

Get your copy at:

Emersonknives.com or TheGuardianShepherd.com

VOLUME II TRAINING

This volume, Training teaches you how to develop your skills to their ultimate potential. Covered here are the drills and exercises needed to supercharge your natural, instinctive, abilities. The topics covered include mastering body mechanics, speed training, and developing Ultimate Power. It also includes detailed sections on developing the proper mindset, the universal rules of combat and the anatomy of a knife attack ending with the Golden Rule of Surviving combat.

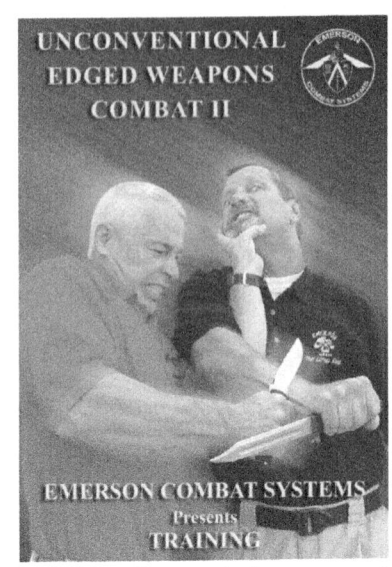

Get your copy at:

Emersonknives.com or TheGuardianShepherd.com

VOLUME III
APPLICATIONS

This is where you learn the tools of the trade. In this third Evolution, Emerson introduces you to all aspects of using the knife as a weapon. Through a series of drills and exercises you will learn how to utilize the principles from foundations and training in actual applications of the knife. Taught here are the strikes, combinations, and techniques including the dynamic art of knife boxing, needed to become a master in the use of a knife and how and when to use them to their maximum potential.

Get your copy at:

Emersonknives.com or TheGuardianShepherd.com

VOLUME IV INTEGRATED WARRIOR

What is the Integrated Warrior Protocol? It is the ability to flow seamlessly between one weapons system and the next. Most arts teach knife techniques, Empty Hand and Grappling as single arts. What happens when you integrate all systems at once? This is the integrated Warrior Protocol. Learn to integrate your knife techniques into your fighting, your boxing, your takedowns and your throws. Learn a system never taught before to the general public and completely revolutionize your fighting ability forever.

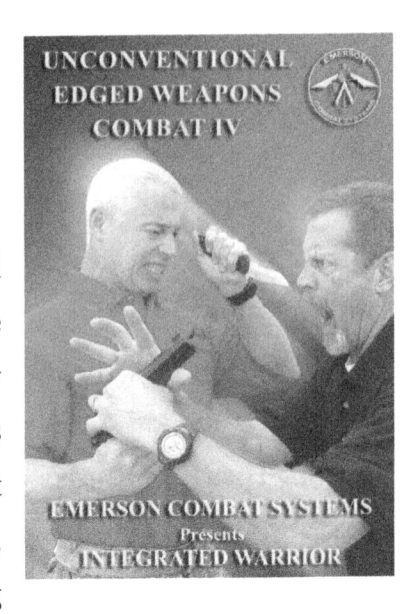

Get your copy at:

Emersonknives.com or TheGuardianShepherd.com

VOLUME V
ADVANCED
TACTICS

Advanced Tactics is where you put everything together. This volume is the culmination of everything taught in Volumes I-IV. Here you will see everything from unarmed techniques against the knife attack, knife against knife, the devastating effectiveness of the "Tiger Gut" and "Buss Saw" and introducing you to the revolutionary and efficient art of knife trapping.

Get your copy at:

Emersonknives.com or TheGuardianShepherd.com

THE COMPLETE COMBAT KARAMBIT

This course introduces you to an entirely new and revolutionary way of fighting with a knife. Developed by Instructor Ernest Emerson to be straightforward, effective, and efficient, this fighting style has to be experienced to be believed. This course is, in large part, the same system that Emerson originated and teaches to elite military units worldwide. This knife fighting style, proven in modern combat, has never been seen by civilian subjects until the release of this course. Modified to exploit the advantages of the Karambit Knife, this amazing fighting system is hard core, bare bones, and brutally effective.

Mr. Emerson teaches a brutal and effective method of fighting that is highly regarded at the highest levels of the U.S. Government and the U.S. Military. Considered a valuable National Asset, Mr. Emerson instructs U.S. Elite Counter - Terrorist Units along with other "Special" Units of the United States Government in the brutal realities of life and death, hand-to-hand Combat.

In this instructional series, The Combat Karambit, you can learn how to use what Mr. Emerson has called one of the best Personal Defense Weapons ever developed - the Karambit Knife. Emerson has taken an age old weapon and thrust it into the 21st century applying his methods of modern, state of the art, combat applications. Now you can learn from the instructor who teaches those considered the Tip of the Spear in America's ongoing war on Terror and are at this moment hunting down and neutralizing those who threaten terror against America.

Get your copy at:

Emersonknives.com or TheGuardianShepherd.com

The Author

Hundreds of books have been published about personal protection, self- defense, conditioning and training, so what makes these so special? Whatever the case, if you are at all like me you are only looking for results. I am a results oriented individual in everything I do and it is driven particularly by how little time I actually have to do anything I want to do. It's the same for you. Without a clear path to results, you'll waste a lot of money and even more valuable, your precious time and in the end walk away disappointed and disillusioned. You'll find that all of these books are designed not so much to teach you something new or to undo what you already know, but instead to enhance the mastery of the skills that you already possess. In essence, to make you more effective, more efficient and to super charge the power that you already have. My goal in everything that I write or teach is to enable that reader or that student to get the absolute most benefit out of their efforts and in the end create an individual who is able to realize the ultimate expression of their performance in these skill sets. Especially if you are ever called to action to use your skills to protect yourself, your loved ones, a teammate, or some other in need of help. It's not so much about what you do, but about being the best at what you do. These books are all written with that goal in mind.

If you go to the web sites – Emerosnknives.com or TheGuardianShepherd.com, you will find access to these and other books by Emerson, along with safety products, self-defense products, the blog, articles, videos, recommendations, and related tips including advice on self-protection and walking the path of a "Warrior

Shepherd," one who will willingly and without hesitation stand in harm's way to protect those who are in need.

Mr. Emerson is a noted author lecturer and teacher. He is a respected historian specializing in Roman and Middle Eastern History.

His athletic background includes a college football scholarship, professional baseball. Boxing, kickboxing, Jeet Kune Do, Filipino KALI and Gracie Jiu Jitsu. He has instructed at most of the major combat and shooting schools in the world including Gun Site, The Crucible, International Tactical Training Seminars, Inc., Blackwater, and is a "plank owner" of the think tank, The Combat Research and Development Group. Mr. Emerson was the lead instructor for the company, Global Studies Group International, (GSGI), a training, security and consulting company run by former members of SEAL Team Six, for over 10 years. He is the founder of the Emerson Combat System and has taught his system to "Tier One" military and law enforcement agencies the world over and he is the owner of the Black Shamrock Combat Academy in Los Angeles California.

Known as the "father of the tactical knife" he is also the owner of Emerson Knives, Inc., which produces the most sought after tactical and combat cutlery in the world. Mr.

Emerson developed the modern tactical knife and has designed the most recognized iconic knife designs in cutlery history. His work has been featured in scores of articles, magazines, movies and T.V. shows. He is one of the few living artists whose work has been on exhibit at both The New York Metropolitan Museum of Art and The Smithsonian in Washington D.C.

Mr. Emerson can be contacted at:
Ernest@emersonknives.com

Made in the USA
Monee, IL
10 November 2020